The Elasticity of Demand for Health Care

A Review of the Literature and Its Application to the Military Health System

Jeanne S. Ringel
Susan D. Hosek
Ben A. Vollaard
Sergej Mahnovski

Prepared for the Office of the Secretary of Defense

National Defense Research Institute | RAND Health

RAND

The research described in this report was sponsored by the Office of the Secretary of Defense (OSD). The research was conducted jointly by RAND Health's Center for Military Health Policy Research and the Forces and Resources Policy Center of the National Defense Research Institute, a federally funded research and development center supported by the OSD, the Joint Staff, the unified commands, and the defense agencies under Contract DASW01-01-C-0004.

ISBN: 0-8330-3109-0

Published 2002 by RAND
1700 Main Street, P.O. Box 2138, Santa Monica, CA 90407-2138
1200 South Hayes Street, Arlington, VA 22202-5050
201 North Craig Street, Suite 102, Pittsburgh, PA 15213-1516
RAND URL: http://www.rand.org/
To order RAND documents or to obtain additional information,
contact Distribution Services: Telephone: (310) 451-7002;
Fax: (310) 451-6915; Email: order@rand.org

PREFACE

This report reviews the health economic research conducted at RAND and elsewhere in an effort to summarize what this research has to say about the elasticity of demand for health care and to consider how this set of results applies to the problem of estimating the demand for health care that is provided by the Department of Defense to military members, their families, and retirees.

The work reported here was sponsored by PA&E and was carried out jointly by RAND Health's Center for Military Health Policy Research and the Forces and Resources Policy Center of the National Defense Research Institute. The latter is a federally funded research and development center sponsored by the Office of the Secretary of Defense, the Joint Staff, the unified commands, and the defense agencies.

CONTENTS

TABLES

Understanding the effects of changes in health insurance policies on the demand for health care services is an important and timely topic. As the Military Health System (MHS) has evolved over time, it has begun to adopt cost-containment strategies that have been tested in private health plans. These strategies have led to changes in many aspects of the health care services offered to Department of Defense (DoD) beneficiaries. Each change potentially can affect the number of people accessing services, the intensity of use, and the cost to the DoD. The goal of this report is to summarize the research relevant for considering the effects of policy changes on the demand for DoD health care services and associated costs.

DIFFERENCES BETWEEN DEMAND FOR HEALTH CARE IN GENERAL AND MILITARY HEALTH CARE

Very little of the existing literature speaks directly to demand for DoD-paid health care, which differs in several important ways from the demand for health care services in general. To use the estimates from the literature to predict the effects of changes in DoD health benefit packages on the use of DoD services, one must understand the differences, which derive from the unusual organizational structure of the MHS. We have identified four key differences. First, active duty personnel have less discretion in seeking care than their civilian counterparts and some military duties involve higher risk. Moreover, to ensure that active duty personnel are healthy and fit for duty, they are provided more frequent preventive and routine care than would be typical for civilians the same age (Hosek et al., 1995).

Changes in MHS benefits can be expected to have little effect on use by active duty personnel.

Second, many retirees and some active duty spouses are eligible for other health insurance (Hosek et al., 1995), usually through their current employers. These beneficiaries may elect not to participate in this other insurance, especially if they must pay a share of the premium. If they do participate, they may obtain their health care through their other insurance, the MHS, or both. Changes in the MHS benefits can be expected to affect both the number of beneficiaries relying on the MHS (rather than on other insurance) and the intensity of service use among all enrollees.

Third, MHS benefits can differ substantially for military treatment facility (MTF) versus civilian care. As a result, government and beneficiary costs depend on both the level of demand and its allocation between the MTFs and civilian providers. Costs in other health plans may also differ according to the mix of providers used, but few vary benefits in the same way that TRICARE does. Studies that estimate the effects of differential benefits on provider choice may be useful in assessing MTF-civilian provider choice in TRICARE.

Fourth, military beneficiaries typically use substantially more health care services than comparable civilians do (Hosek et al., 1995). This difference may be due to better benefits in the MHS. If this is so, the general health demand literature may be safely applied because use by the military is described by the same demand curve as use by the general population, but with the two groups positioned at different points on the curve. Alternatively, differences in use might reflect different demand responses to the same benefits. In this case, the demand curves differ and the general literature may not be applicable. There is some reason for believing the first explanation. A large share of active duty personnel and their families receive care free of charge at MTFs. Out-of-pocket costs for those using civilian care appear to be no more than costs in other plans (Levy et al., 2000).

Although there are a variety of differences between the demand for health care in general and the demand for DoD health care specifically, the existing empirical research on the demand for health care, on the demand for health insurance, and on the choice of providers offers useful information about how people respond to changes in the price of health care. The differences outlined above merely provide a framework for applying the existing estimates to the unique situations faced by DoD.

THE ELASTICITY OF DEMAND

The elasticity of demand is a measure of the responsiveness of product demand to changes in one of its determinants. The demand determinants for which elasticity measures are typically computed are the price of the good or service, the income of the consumer, and the prices of related goods or services. Elasticity measures are particularly useful because they focus on the relative magnitudes of changes rather than the absolute. As such, elasticity measures are free of units of measurement. This characteristic makes them particularly useful for comparing demand responses across products, countries, and individuals.

RESULTS

Elasticity of Demand for Health Care in General

Despite a wide variety of empirical methods and data sources, the demand for health care is consistently found to be price inelastic. Although the range of price elasticity estimates is relatively wide, it tends to center on –0.17, meaning that a 1 percent increase in the price of health care will lead to a 0.17 percent reduction in health care expenditures. The price-induced changes in demand for health care can in large part be attributed to changes in the probability of accessing any care rather than to changes in the number of visits once care has been accessed. In addition, the studies consistently find lower levels of demand elasticity at lower levels of cost-sharing.

The demand for health is also found to be income inelastic. The estimates of income elasticity of demand are in the range of 0 to 0.2. The positive sign of the elasticity measure indicates that as income increases, the demand for health care services also increases. The magnitude of the elasticity, however, suggests that the demand response is relatively small. Studies based on long time series data tend to report higher income elasticities. The difference in estimates across time frames is due to the incorporation of the effects of changes in medical technology in studies that use long time series of data.

Elasticity of Demand for Specific Classes of Health Care Services

Although the price elasticity of demand for medical care in general is relatively low, certain types of care are found to be somewhat more price sensitive. Preventive care and pharmacy benefits are among those medical services with larger price elasticities. The finding that the demand for preventive care is more price sensitive than the demand for other types of care is not surprising. The number of available substitutes for a product is a major determinant of demand elasticity. In the case of preventive care, a number of goods and services could possibly serve as substitutes. As a result, when the price of care increases, consumers are able to substitute away from preventive care toward other goods and services that promote health such as nutritional supplements and healthy foods. In addition, preventive medical services may be seen more as a luxury than a necessity and, thus, may be put off when the price of such care increases. Further, the opportunity cost of obtaining preventive care is much higher than it is when the patient is sick, particularly if the illness keeps the individual out of work. It is also likely, that since the benefits of preventive care accrue in the long-term, they are heavily discounted. The difference in elasticities may also reflect the fact that preventive care and prescription drugs are typically not as well covered by insurance.

Elasticity of Demand for Health Insurance

Apart from studies on the responsiveness of the demand for health care to price and income, there is growing attention to the responsiveness of demand for different health plans to changes in the price of insurance. This literature is of particular importance when considering the demand for health care services provided by a particular health plan. Any change in the out-of-pocket costs of services or premium costs will have an effect on the number of plan enrollees and, thus, on the demand for health care services paid for by that plan.

According to Royalty and Solomon (1998), "there is no definitely established range of price elasticities [of health plan choice] in the literature." Econometric studies of health care plan choice vary dramatically not only in their price elasticity estimates but also in the data sources, econometric methods, and experimental design. For example, the articles reviewed in this report use datasets of individual employees and their health plan choices in various professional and demographic settings, such as a single university, 20 firms within one city, a single company with four plants across the United States, and a national cross-section, among others. Based on this literature, the estimates of the elasticity of the demand for health insurance with respect to price range between –1.8 and –0.1.

USING ESTIMATES FROM THE LITERATURE TO PREDICT THE EFFECTS OF CHANGES IN THE MHS SYSTEM

The FY 2001 National Defense Authorization Act was signed into law by President Clinton on October 30, 2000. Although the act contains numerous changes, four new TRICARE initiatives will have important effects on uniformed services retirees and their spouses.

- Expanding pharmacy benefits for seniors to include access to MTF pharmacies, the National Mail Order Pharmacy Program, and retail pharmacies,

- Making TRICARE a second payer to Medicare (TRICARE for Life),

- Eliminating coinsurance payments under TRICARE Prime for dependents of active duty personnel, and

- Expanding TRICARE Prime Remote benefits to active duty family members and nonuniformed service members.

All of these new initiatives expand services and reduce the costs of health care for some group of MHS beneficiaries. Consequently, we would expect to see greater demand for MHS services as these policies are implemented. For example, expanding pharmacy benefits to seniors will likely increase the demand for pharmaceuticals paid for by MHS as Medicare-eligible beneficiaries who previously paid out-of-pocket for prescriptions will now get them through the TRICARE program. In addition, the reduction in the price of prescriptions will induce some beneficiaries to purchase a greater number of prescriptions. Estimates from the literature indicate that a 10 percent decrease in the price of prescriptions will lead to a 2 to 3 percent increase in the quantity demanded. These estimates, however, likely understate the change in demand that the DoD will face because they reflect only the change in the number of prescriptions among current enrollees and not the change in the number of enrollees.

Similarly, making TRICARE a second payer to Medicare is expected to increase demand for MHS paid services. Studies have shown that health care use is higher among the elderly who have Medigap (or supplemental) insurance (for examples, see Link et al., 1980; Christensen et al., 1987; McCall et al., 1991, Cartwright et al., 1992). This new initiative will make TRICARE for Life a close substitute for other Medigap policies. Although none of the previous studies calculate an elasticity of demand specifically for Medicare recipients, we believe that the estimates for adults in general serve as a lower bound. The elderly are expected to have a more elastic demand for health care services, since they typically have more limited incomes and spend a greater share of that income on health care needs.

In the case of TRICARE Prime, the elimination of copayments for civilian care provided to active duty dependents will increase the demand for MHS-paid medical services in two ways. First, the economic literature predicts that reductions in copayments will increase the number of current enrollees who access any care, particularly among those who rely on civilian providers. The literature also indicates, however, that the price elasticity of demand for health care is relatively low at low levels of cost-sharing (see Newhouse et al. 1993). The current copayments for active duty dependents are relatively low, thus the effect of eliminating these copayments may be relatively small. The second effect is that some beneficiaries may choose to switch between TRICARE plans. The lower out-of-pocket costs for civilian care may make the Prime option more attractive to families that had previously chosen the Extra or Standard TRICARE options. The literature on the elasticity of health care plan choice suggests that some switching between plans does occur in response to changes in plan characteristics. The magnitude of such effects, however, has not been well established.

The expansion of the TRICARE Prime Remote benefits to dependents of active duty personnel and uniformed service personnel (i.e., personnel from the Public Health Service, the Coast Guard, and the National Oceanic and Atmospheric Administration) will likely increase the demand for health care services paid through the TRICARE program. Most of the affected beneficiaries must now use TRICARE Standard, which imposes significant copayments. The reduction in out-of-pocket costs may increase the demand for care, especially if Prime cost-control mechanisms are less effective for this dispersed population than they are for more concentrated populations.

ACKNOWLEDGMENTS

We wish to thank Ross Anthony and Susan Everingham for their thoughtful comments and suggestions throughout the project. In addition, Katherine Harris provided valuable comments on an earlier draft of this report. Her suggestions have greatly improved the final product.

Chapter One

INTRODUCTION

Understanding the effects of changes in health insurance policies on the demand for health care services is an important and timely topic. As the Military Health System (MHS) has evolved over time, it has begun to adopt cost-containment strategies that have been tested in private health plans. These strategies have led to changes in many aspects of the health care services offered to Department of Defense (DoD) beneficiaries. Each change can potentially affect the number of people accessing services, the intensity of use, and the cost to the DoD.

In this report, we review the extensive economic literature that seeks to explain how changes in health insurance policies will affect health care use and the overall cost of providing services. The economic literature typically measures such effects as demand elasticities—i.e., how responsive consumer demand is to changes in the good's own price, the consumer's income, or the price of related goods. It is our hope that the review of the existing literature on health care demand elasticity will provide a greater understanding of the effects of price changes on the demand that the DoD faces. Such an understanding is extremely important when evaluating the effects of new or proposed changes in DoD health plans. Several such changes are being implemented as directed by the FY 2001 National Defense Authorization Act that was signed into law by President Clinton on October 30, 2000. These initiatives will

- Expand pharmacy benefits for seniors to include access to military treatment facility (MTF) pharmacies, the National Mail Order Pharmacy Program, and retail pharmacies,

- Make TRICARE (the military health plan) a second payer to Medicare,

- Eliminate coinsurance payments under TRICARE Prime (the health maintenance organization (HMO) option) for dependents of active duty personnel, and

- Expand TRICARE Prime Remote to active duty family members and nonuniformed service members.

This report summarizes the research relevant for considering the effects of policy changes on the demand for DoD health care services and the associated costs. After reviewing the literature, we return to these policy changes and discuss how the results from the existing literature can be used to predict the effects of such changes on use and costs.

Very little of the existing literature speaks directly to demand for DoD-paid health care, which differs in several important ways from the demand for health care services in general. To use the estimates from the literature to predict the effects of changes in DoD health benefit packages on the use of DoD services, one must understand the differences, which derive from the unusual organizational structure of the MHS.

A BRIEF DESCRIPTION OF THE MILITARY HEALTH SYSTEM

The MHS provides health care coverage to a wide spectrum of beneficiaries, including active duty military personnel and their dependents, retired military personnel and their dependents, and survivors of military personnel. Over the past 15 years, as the active duty force has been reduced by one-third, the mix of beneficiaries served by the MHS has shifted away from active duty personnel toward other beneficiaries. In fact, family members and retirees now make up approximately 80 percent of the population covered by the MHS (GAO, 2000).

In response to growing health care costs, DoD decided to make changes in the MHS that mirrored those taking place in the civilian sector. In the mid-1990s, DoD implemented a new managed-care plan, called TRICARE. TRICARE offers three benefit options. The first is TRICARE Prime, an HMO in which all care is provided in MTFs or by a network of civilian providers. All active duty personnel are automatically enrolled in Prime and receive most of their care in the MTFs. Beneficiaries who choose not to enroll in TRICARE Prime are eligible for MTF care on a space-available basis and have two options for civilian care: TRICARE Standard, a fee-for-service option with the same benefits as the pre-TRICARE civilian program (CHAMPUS) and TRICARE Extra, a preferred provider organization (PPO) that provides enhanced benefits when care is provided by the same civilian provider network used for Prime.

These civilian-care options are provided to retirees and their dependents until they become eligible for Medicare at age 65. Medicare then replaces TRICARE as the payer for civilian care, but these beneficiaries remain eligible for MTF care so long as there is space available. Base closures and a shift in MTF priorities to Prime enrollees have meant that less space is available for Medicare-eligible beneficiaries. Since Medicare benefits are not comparable to TRICARE benefits, the loss of MTF access has resulted in an erosion of benefits for this group. Recently, Congress extended TRICARE eligibility to Medicare-eligible beneficiaries, beginning October 1, 2001.[1] We discuss this change further in Chapter Four.

Tables 1.1 and 1.2, which are taken from the TRICARE Handbook (www.tricare.osd.mil), summarize the benefits available for nonactive duty beneficiaries under age 65 in the different plans before the implementation of the FY 2001 National Defense Authorization Act. DoD pays the full cost of all health care for active duty personnel.

KEY DIFFERENCES BETWEEN THE MILITARY AND CIVILIAN HEALTH SYSTEMS

Military and civilian health care demand differs for several reasons. First, active duty personnel have less discretion in seeking care than their civilian counterparts and some military duties involve higher risk. To ensure that active duty personnel are healthy and fit for duty, they are provided more frequent preventive and routine care

---

[1]Eligibility for additional prescription benefits was initiated six months earlier.

Table 1.1

TRICARE Benefits for Active Duty Family Members

	TRICARE Prime E-1 to E-4	TRICARE Prime E-5 and Up	TRICARE Extra	TRICARE Standard
Annual deductible	None	None	$150/individual or $300/family for E-5 and above; $50/$100 for E-4 & below	$150/individual or $300/family for E-5 and above; $50/$100 for E-4 and below
Civilian outpatient visit	$6/visit	$12/visit	15% of negotiated fee	20% of allowable charge
Civilian inpatient admission	$11/day ($25 min.)	$11/day ($25 min.)	Greater of $25 or $10.85/day	Greater of $25 or $10.85/day
Civilian inpatient mental health	$20/day	$20/day	$20/day	$20/day

Table 1.2

TRICARE Benefits for Retirees, Their Dependents, and Others Under Age 65

	TRICARE Prime	TRICARE Extra	TRICARE Standard
Annual deductible	None	$150/individual or $300/family	$150/individual or $300/family
Annual enrollment fees	$230/individual or $460/family	None	None
Civilian provider copays:		20% of negotiated fee	25% of allowable charge
Outpatient	$12		
Emergency	$30		
Mental health	$25 ($17 for group visit)		
Civilian inpatient cost share	$11/day ($25 min.)	Lesser of $250/day or 25% of negotiated charges plus 20% of negotiated professional fees	25% of billed charges plus 25% of allowed professional fees

than would be typical for civilians the same age (Hosek et al., 1995).[2] Changes in TRICARE benefits can be expected to have little effect on use by active duty personnel and analyses of demand in the military system do not apply standard demand research to this group.

Second, many retirees and some active duty spouses are eligible for other health insurance (Hosek et al., 1995), usually through their current employers. These beneficiaries may elect not to participate in this other insurance, especially if they must pay a share of the premium. If they do participate, they may obtain their health care through their other insurance, TRICARE, or both. Changes in TRICARE will induce changes in the number of beneficiaries who rely on TRICARE (rather than other insurance) as well as the demand for care in TRICARE. Thus, the availability of outside health insurance options makes the demand for DoD health care services more elastic than the demand for health care in general. Since a number of beneficiaries use TRICARE to supplement their other insurance, the effects of changes in TRICARE can be very complex. Dual coverage is very rare in the general population, so the literature on the effects of health plan changes typically disregards these dual-coverage issues. However, by appropriately combining results from both the health care and health insurance demand literatures, the more complex military health demand effects can be analyzed.

Third, as Tables 1.1 and 1.2 illustrate, TRICARE benefits can differ substantially for MTF versus civilian care. As a result, government and beneficiary costs depend on both the level of demand and its allocation between the MTFs and civilian providers. Costs in other health plans may also differ according to the mix of providers used, but few vary benefits in the same way that TRICARE does.

Fourth, military beneficiaries typically use substantially more health care services than comparable civilians do (Hosek et al., 1995). This difference may be due to better benefits in the MHS. If so, the general health demand literature may be safely applied because use by the military is described by the same demand curve as use by the

---

[2]For example, enlisted personnel (except senior ones) have no sick leave. They must go to "sick call" to be excused from duty, even for the most routine illnesses. Other personnel, such as pilots and undersea divers, must be certified fit for duty even if they have only minor health problems (e.g., a cold).

general population, but the two groups are positioned at different points on the curve. Alternatively, differences in use might reflect different demand responses to the same benefits. In this case, the demand curves differ and the general literature may not be applicable. There is some reason for believing the first explanation. A large share of active duty personnel and their families receive care free of charge at MTFs. Out-of-pocket costs for those using civilian care appear to be no more than costs in other plans (Levy et al., 2000).[3] Therefore, average out-of-pocket costs for health care services are lower in the MHS and we would expect to see higher use among DoD beneficiaries. However, there may be other explanations for the higher levels of use that could imply different demand elasticities. One such explanation is differing patterns of medical practice between the military and civilian health care systems. MTF resources during the time period under study by Hosek et al. depended on historical use. As such, MTF commanders had little incentive to keep use and costs down. They often also lacked the personnel and space for efficient clinical practice.[4] Similarly, differences in access to care might alter demand elasticities, but recent data suggest that access in the MHS is similar to access in civilian health plans.

As we indicated above, the DoD beneficiaries include retired personnel who are eligible for Medicare. These beneficiaries have been eligible only for MTF care, but TRICARE will also supplement their Medicare coverage for civilian care beginning in FY 2001. Most studies of health care demand and its sensitivity to price change deal with the nonelderly population. Although there is not a great deal of empirical evidence on the relative magnitudes of the elasticity of demand for health care between elderly and nonelderly populations, economic theory does provide some predictions. Theory suggests that the elasticity of demand for a product increases as its budget share grows. In other words, the demand for products that make up a large portion of an individual's budget is expected to be more sensitive to changes in price. Health care services can be expected to

---

[3]As we discuss in Chapter Four, cost-sharing for active duty dependents will decrease in FY 2002.

[4]The MHS Optimization Plan spells out a broad set of changes that will be implemented between now and 2007 to enhance the cost effectiveness of its health care delivery system.

make up a larger share of the total budget for the elderly than for the nonelderly. The elderly health care budget share is likely to be larger because the elderly use considerably more health care services than the nonelderly. As a result, we would expect the elasticity of demand for health care to be larger for the elderly than for the nonelderly.

Although there are a variety of differences between the demand for health care in general and the demand for DoD health care specifically, the existing empirical research on the demand for health care, on the demand for health insurance, and on the choice of providers offers useful information about how people respond to changes in the price of health care. The differences outlined above merely provide a framework for applying the existing estimates to the unique situations faced by DoD.

The remainder of the report is organized as follows. First, we briefly explain what is meant by the term "elasticity of demand" and describe how it can be measured. We then discuss the three main methodologies that appear in the literature, pointing out the advantages and disadvantages of each. Chapter Three contains the literature review. We begin the review by discussing the elasticity of demand for health care services in general. We then present estimates for specific types of services such as preventive care, inpatient care, and pharmacy. We also describe the literature on health insurance demand. In Chapter Four, we consider potential changes to the MHS and discuss how the estimates taken from the economic literature may help to predict the effects of such changes.

Chapter Two

METHODS

DESCRIPTION OF ELASTICITY MEASURES

The demand for a product summarizes the relationship between the quantity of the good or service desired and the price at which it is offered for sale. Besides the price of the good, many factors such as the prices of related goods, changing tastes and preferences, consumer income, or expectations about the future influence the demand for a particular product. The elasticity of demand is a measure of the responsiveness of product demand to changes in one of these determinants. The demand determinants for which elasticity measures are typically computed are the price of the good or service, the income of the consumer, and the prices of related goods or services. Elasticity measures are particularly useful because they focus on the relative magnitudes of changes rather than the absolute. As such, elasticity measures are free of units of measurement. This characteristic makes them particularly useful for comparing demand responses across products, countries, and individuals.

Own-Price Elasticity of Demand

Price elasticity of demand measures the percentage change in quantity demanded resulting from a 1 percent change in price. The value of the elasticity of demand for a product varies depending on the level of price and quantity at which it is evaluated. In other words, at different combinations of price and quantity demanded, the elasticity of demand for a particular product can vary significantly. As a convention, elasticity measures reported in the literature are typically evaluated at the mean value of price and quantity in the data used in the estimation. In practice, the price elasticity of demand will always be negative. This indicates that as the price of a good increases all other factors held constant, consumers will demand less of that good. The magnitude of the elasticity estimate provides a measure of how responsive demand is. If the value of the price elasticity estimate is greater than one in absolute value, then demand is said to be elastic. When demand is elastic, consumers are very responsive to changes in price. As such, a small price change will lead to a relatively large change in quantity demanded. In contrast, if the value of the elasticity of demand estimate is less than one in absolute value, then demand is said to be inelastic and consumers are not very responsive to price changes. The demand for health care services is expected to be relatively inelastic, in large part because there are few close substitutes for medical services.

Income Elasticity of Demand

The income elasticity of demand measures how responsive consumers are to changes in their level of income. It is measured as the ratio of the percentage change in quantity demanded to the percentage change in income. The demand for a product can be income elastic, where consumer demand is very responsive to income changes, or income inelastic, where income changes have very little effect on demand. The characteristics of a product can help to predict the magnitude of income elasticities. Products that are necessities are expected to be relatively income inelastic, whereas the demand for discretionary goods is expected to be relatively responsive to changes in income. Classifying health care services in general into the category of necessity or discretionary is quite difficult. There is wide variation across medical services with some, such as treatment for a heart attack, clearly classified as necessities and others, such as cosmetic surgery, clearly considered luxuries. Certainly, many types of services fall somewhere in between. Whether health care demand is elastic or inelastic with respect to income is an empirical question that has spurred a large literature.

Cross-Price Elasticity of Demand

The cross-price elasticity measures the effect of a change in the price of one good or service on the demand for another product. For example, it could be used to measure the percentage change in the quantity of product x demanded resulting from a 1 percent change in the price of product y. The sign of the cross-price elasticity depends on the relationship between the two products. If the goods are substitutes in use then the cross-price elasticity will be positive. The positive sign reflects the fact that as the price of one good goes up the demand for a substitute good will increase as consumers switch away from the product that has become relatively more expensive. In contrast, if two goods are complements in use, goods that are used together, then the cross-price elasticity of demand between them will be negative. When the price of one good goes up the demand for the other will fall. The consideration of cross-price elasticities will be most prevalent when we discuss the elasticity of demand for specific types of medical services.

SPECIAL ISSUES REGARDING THE ELASTICITY OF DEMAND FOR HEALTH

The demand for health is somewhat more complicated than the demand for a typical product and estimating the elasticity of demand for health is less straightforward. In this section we outline the important considerations when estimating health care demand elasticities.

Measures of Health Care Demand

Consumers have demand for health but cannot directly purchase it. They must purchase health care services that are used to produce health. The idea that health care has a derived, rather than a direct, demand was first discussed by Michael Grossman in an article published in 1972.

The amount of health care demanded is sometimes measured by the quantity of services used, such as inpatient days, outpatient visits, or prescriptions. More often, it is measured by the total cost of the services, allowing for the combination of services measured in different quantity units. Either measure can be used to estimate standard demand elasticities.

DoD is typically interested in determining the effects of policy and other changes on its costs. Most studies do not express elasticities in terms of insurer costs. Elasticities measured for total costs and insurer costs are not necessarily equal, particularly when the health plan has a deductible and out-of-pocket cap. In using estimates of elasticities from the literature, the DoD analyst must be careful to apply them correctly.

Price of Health Care

The price schedule for health care services is quite complex. The price that a consumer pays for health care services depends on the presence of a cost-sharing plan (coinsurance rates or copayments), a deductible, an upper limit on out-of-pocket expenditures, and premiums. As such, the price of health services can vary according to the quantity of services used. This makes the estimation of the price elasticity of demand for health care services somewhat difficult. To estimate the true effect of price changes the researcher must be able to determine the effective price that the consumer would pay for an additional unit of health services. As an example, it seems likely that an individual who has reached his or her out-of-pocket expenditure cap for the year and thus faces a price of zero will make different choices about health care use than someone who has not yet reached his or her deductible and thus faces the full price of health care services. The complexity of the price schedule highlights the importance of understanding the context in which an elasticity is estimated when trying to generalize results from the literature.

Time Prices and Health Care

One portion of the cost of any product is the time it takes to purchase it. With medical care, the time price can be very important. The waiting time associated with seeing a physician can have a significant effect on the demand for health care services. Waiting times are often categorized into time waiting to obtain an appointment and time spent waiting in the physician's office. In general, the literature on the effect of time prices on health care demand focuses primarily on the time spent waiting in the office. This distinction is often made because, while the individual waits in the physician's office, he or she cannot work (or do other activities) and thus faces an important tradeoff.

In a system where the out-of-pocket cost to the consumer is very low or zero, time prices can still ration the use of medical services. Only those for whom the benefits of medical service outweigh the time costs will choose to visit the doctor. As a result, we would expect to see individuals with a lower opportunity cost of time using more medical services than those with high opportunity costs of time.[1] Theory predicts that own-time price elasticities will be negative and cross-price time elasticities will be positive. The negative own-time price elasticity indicates that as waiting times increase, the demand for medical services will fall. As such, it is important to consider the full costs of medical care, monetary plus time costs, when studying health care demand.

Types of Health Care

The types of health care services offered vary widely and we might expect that the elasticity of demand for specific service types would vary as well. The demand for inpatient services could respond differently to price changes than the demand for outpatient services. Similarly, we might expect differences in the responsiveness of demand for acute and preventive care. Further, health care services can include lab work, office visits, pharmaceuticals, x-rays, and a variety of other goods and services. This heterogeneity suggests that estimating separate demand elasticities for each category of health services could be quite informative.

---

[1]The individual's market wage is often used as a proxy for the opportunity cost of time.

Interrelationships Between the Demand for Health Insurance and Health Care

Understanding the demand for health care paid for by a particular health plan is somewhat more complex than understanding the demand for health care in general. When considering the demand faced by an individual plan, there are two important effects of any change in the out-of-pocket costs of medical services. First, if the out-of-pocket costs for care in a particular health plan fall, more consumers will choose to join that insurance plan. Additionally, the decrease in cost will lead those already enrolled in the plan to use more services than before. Therefore, the change in quantity of services provided resulting from a price change is a combination of changes in these factors. The total effect of a price change on the demand for health care services paid for by a particular insurance plan can be seen as the sum of two separate elasticities. The first captures the effect on demand of changes in the number of enrollees in the health insurance plan. The second represents the effect of the change in price on the demand for medical services among current enrollees.

Much of the work on the elasticity of demand for health care has focused on the change in medical services among enrollees.[2] As such, estimates of that portion of the elasticity receive more attention in our summary of the literature. The implication of this for understanding the demand that the DoD faces is that estimates from the literature will tend to understate the effect of any change in the out-of-pocket costs of health care for DoD beneficiaries. In recent years there has been a growing literature on the demand for health insurance. The final section of the literature review in Chapter Three summarizes this recent work and presents estimates of the effect of price changes on the demand for a particular health plan. In combination, these two sets of estimates provide a fuller picture of health care demand in a particular health plan.

Determining the change in insurer costs associated with a change in health care demand requires more information if the health plan

---

[2]Estimates of the effect on demand of changes in the number of services used among current enrollees are obtained from studies of the elasticity of demand for health care in general where the design of the study focuses on individuals who do not change health plans.

employs a deductible and out-of-pocket cap. The change in demand should be determined separately for individuals who do not exceed the deductible, who exceed the deductible but not the cap, and who exceed the cap. The insurer's cost share will then differ for these three groups. The analyst may also need to consider changes in demand for different providers if the plan's cost-sharing or the providers' costs differ for the same care. All of these complications apply to TRICARE.

Selection Effects

Adverse selection is an important consideration in the estimation of demand elasticities for health care. Adverse selection occurs when persons with poor health tend to choose insurance with high benefits and persons with good health tend to avoid such insurance because of its high cost. If adverse selection is present, elasticity estimates will measure the difference in needs of people with different health and socioeconomic status in addition to the quantity response to the price change. In some cases, researchers have been interested in measuring the degree of adverse selection, using sophisticated statistical techniques to decompose the total effect on demand.

Moral Hazard

Estimating the demand for health care is further complicated by the presence of moral hazard. Ex ante moral hazard occurs when the presence of insurance undermines an individual's incentives to take actions to help prevent a loss. Ex post moral hazard comes into play after the injury or illness has already occurred. The presence of insurance shields the consumer from paying for the full cost of medical services. As a result, the individual consumes more medical services than he would if he had no insurance (Zweifel and Manning, 2000). It is particularly important, therefore, for researchers to understand the role that moral hazard plays in increasing the demand for medical care services. Any change in price will change the incentives that the individual faces. For example, as the out-of-pocket costs to an individual fall, he or she bears less of the burden of any health care service that is used. As a result, individuals demand more health care services. Estimates of the price elasticity of demand for health care in the literature will incorporate the effects of moral hazard.

Provider Behavior

Estimating the demand for health care services is a complex process that must consider both the consumer's response to changes in price and the provider's ability to induce demand (Weiner, 1993). Physicians may change their patterns of practice, perhaps prescribing more intense treatments, when increased cost-sharing leads to lower demand for their services. Furthermore, physicians act as an agent once care is initiated by the patient and may not consider price in the same way as the patient would.

Chapter Three

REVIEW OF THE EMPIRICAL LITERATURE

In this chapter, we provide an overview of the empirical literature on the elasticity of demand for health care and for health insurance. First, we discuss briefly the empirical methodologies that are used in the literature. Then, we focus upon the results from studies of the demand for health care. We discuss studies that seek to identify a relationship between factors such as income and the price of health care and the use of health care services. In the final section, we examine the demand for health insurance and we discuss studies on the relationship between enrollment decisions and changes in the price of health care insurance.

THE ELASTICITY OF DEMAND FOR HEALTH CARE SERVICES

There is an extensive literature in economics that seeks to estimate the elasticity of demand for health care services. The seminal works in this area were produced during the 1970s and to a large extent have withstood the test of time. Although many of the studies that will be discussed in this section also estimate elasticities for specific services, we choose to focus only on the elasticity of demand for health care services more generally at this point. The elasticities of demand for specific types of medical services will be summarized in the following section.

Methodologies Used in the Literature

The ideal empirical data for estimating the elasticity of demand for health care would include detailed information on personal characteristics, use of medical services, and the effective price paid for an additional unit of health care. Most important, in the ideal data, the observed variations in price and subsequent use would be exogenous. The ideal data, however, do not generally exist. Consequently, researchers have developed a variety of methodologies that can address many of the issues that arise from the lack of ideal data. The methodologies typically used in the literature can be classified into three general categories: experimental, quasi-experimental, and observational. Experimental studies use random assignment into treatment and control groups to infer the effects of a particular treatment (Cook and Campbell, 1979). Estimates from experiments are thought to provide a "gold standard" because the randomization of people into different treatments avoids the problem of selection bias in that individuals under study are not able to choose whether to obtain the treatment. However, there are some disadvantages associated with experimental studies. They can be difficult to design and implement. In addition, they are extremely costly and take a lot of time. It can be many years from the time the experiment starts until the effects can be fully evaluated. Most important for the purposes of this review, the results from experimental studies may not necessarily be generalizable. The effects that are measured in a closely controlled setting may not reflect what will happen upon wider implementation.

The second category of studies of the elasticity of demand for health care is quasi-experiments. These studies are similar to experiments in that there are treatments and outcome measures; however, in quasi-experiments individuals are not randomly assigned to treatment and control groups (Cook and Campbell, 1979). In the case of health care demand, the majority of quasi-experimental studies can be more narrowly defined as natural experiments. Natural experiments identify the effects of treatment using exogenous variations that occur in the economic environment. For example, Cherkin et al. (1989) used the introduction of copayments in the Group Health Cooperative of Puget Sound to estimate the effect of price on the demand for health care services. Comparisons of use before and after the policy change provide the basis for this methodology. The main issue of concern is that the researcher must be able to control for all other factors that may have changed at the same time. If not, the estimated effect of the policy change will incorporate the effects of all of the other unobserved factors that changed during the time period of analysis. As an example, suppose that there was a significant flu epidemic in the year after a health insurance plan change that implemented copayments. Further assume that no change in use is observed after the plan is implemented. At first blush, one could conclude that copayments do not affect demand for health care. This conclusion is flawed, however. The change in use, or lack thereof, reflects both the effect of the change in copayments and the effect of the difference between the incidence of the flu in the pre and post time periods. To obtain estimates of the true effect of the policy change, the researcher must be able to control for other factors that could have affected use during the time period of analysis. In many cases, a comparison group (similar to the control group in the experimental design) that does not receive the policy change is used to help address the question of what would have occurred had the policy not been changed. The extent to which the researcher was able to control for confounding factors must be considered when interpreting results based on natural experiments.

The final category in the literature is observational studies of the elasticity of demand for health care. These studies are often based on survey or administrative data. In such cases, econometric models are used to estimate the demand for health care. The effect of price on the demand for health services is identified from the variation in price across health plans and over time. It can be very difficult to identify causal effects of treatment using observational study methods. Observed correlations between treatment and outcome measures do not necessarily imply causality. As a result, complicated models have been developed to deal with the problems associated with nonexperimental data such as omitted variables, unobserved heterogeneity, selection bias, and endogeneity. These statistical procedures, however, are not feasible in some cases and, thus, the question of causality may not be answered in all observational studies. There are several advantages associated with the use of observational studies. First, they are much less costly to implement than experimental studies and can provide results more quickly. Second, in some cases random assignment into treatment may not be ethical. This is particularly true in the case of health care where randomization into the control group might mean that an individual does not receive a lifesaving treatment. Most important for the purposes of applying results from the literature, the results from observational studies may be more generalizable than results from experiments.

Main Findings

Despite a wide variety of empirical methods and data sources, the estimates of the demand for health care, shown in Table 3.1, are consistently found to be price inelastic. Although the range of price elasticity estimates is relatively wide, it tends to center on –0.17, meaning that a 1 percent increase in the price of health care will lead to a 0.17 percent reduction in health care expenditures. The price-induced changes in demand for health care can in large part be attributed to changes in the probability of accessing any care rather than to changes in the number of visits once care has been accessed. In addition, the studies consistently find lower levels of demand elasticity at lower levels of cost-sharing.

The demand for health is also found to be income inelastic. The estimates of income elasticity of demand are in the range of 0 to 0.2. The positive sign of the elasticity measure indicates that as income increases, the demand for health care services also increases. The magnitude of the elasticity, however, suggests that the demand response is relatively small. Studies based on long time series data tend to report higher income elasticities. The difference in estimates across time frames is due to the incorporation of the effects of changes in medical technology in studies that use long time series data.

Price Elasticity of Demand for Health Care

The price schedule for health care services can be quite complicated. As noted above, the effective price that a consumer pays depends on many factors including coinsurance, deductibles, upper limits on out-of-pocket expenditures, premiums, and the price of the good or service itself. A change in any of these factors will affect the out-of-pocket costs of health care to the consumer. In the summary of the literature below, for each study that is discussed we will identify the source of price variation.

Table 3.1

Key Studies with Price Elasticities for All Services

Study	Methodology	Data/ Population	Price Measure	Quantity Measure	Price Elasticity
Feldstein, 1971	Observational: time-series regression	AHA survey of hospitals, 1958–1967; NCHS survey, 1963–1964	Coinsurance rates and plan generosity	Mean hospital stay	–0.49
Fuchs and Kramer, 1972	Observational: instrumental variables	1966 IRS tabulations	Coinsurance rates and plan generosity	Visits per capita	–0.10 to –0.36
Scitovsky and Snyder, 1972	Natural experiment	Palo Alto Group Health Plan, 1966–1968	Coinsurance rates	Physician visits	–0.14
Rosett and Huang, 1973	Observational: cross-sectional tobit	Survey of Consumer Expenditures, 1960	Out-of-pocket costs	Medical expenditures	–0.35 to –1.5
Beck, 1974	Natural experiment	Sample of low-income people in Saskatchewan, Canada	Copayments	Physician visits	–0.07
Phelps and Newhouse, 1974	Observational	Insurance plans in the United States, United Kingdom, and Canada	Coinsurance rates	Medical expenditures	–0.04 to –0.12
Scitovsky and McCall, 1977	Natural experiment	Palo Alto Group Health Plan, 1968–1972	Coinsurance rates	Physician visits	–0.29
Wedig, 1988	Observational	NMCUES, 1980	Out-of-pocket costs	Physician visits	–0.16 to –0.35
Cherkin et al., 1989	Natural experiment	Group Health Cooperative of Puget Sound	Copayments	Physician visits	–0.04
Newhouse et al., 1993	Experimental	RAND HIE	Coinsurance rates across plans	Medical expenditures	–0.17 to –0.22
Eichner, 1998	Observational: tobit regressions	Insurance claims for those covered through a large employer	Out-of-pocket costs	Medical expenditures	–0.62 to –0.75

The quantity of health care can be measured in a number of ways. In the studies that we review, the number of physician visits and total medical expenditures are the two quantity measures that are predominantly used. In the discussion of each study, as well as in the summary table, we will identify the health care quantity measure that the reported price elasticity estimate is based on. This is important to keep in mind when comparing the elasticity estimates across studies.

Feldstein conducted one of the earliest studies on the price elasticity of demand for health care in 1971. The results were based on micro data at the hospital level and were the first of this type to be considered statistically robust. The data for the study were taken from the American Hospital Association Survey of Hospitals between 1958 and 1967. The effect of price on mean length of stay for hospitalized patients was identified in a time series regression using variations in the price of hospital stays, coinsurance rates, and proportion of the population insured across states. Feldstein estimated that the price elasticity of demand for health care was approximately –0.5. This elasticity estimate is interpreted to say that a 1 percent increase in the coinsurance rate will lead to a 0.5 percent reduction in the mean hospital stay, or that the demand for health care services is relatively inelastic. A later study by Feldstein (1973) used state-level data to estimate a two-stage least squares model and obtained a slightly larger price elasticity estimate of –0.67. The two-stage estimation procedure was used in an effort to control for the potential endogeneity of the price of insurance.

In a similar vein, Fuchs and Kramer (1972) used aggregate state-level data to investigate the price elasticity of demand for health care services. The estimates of the elasticity based on net prices ranged between –0.15 and –0.20, which are substantially smaller than the estimates from Feldstein (1971, 1973). These results indicate that the demand for physician visits is relatively insensitive to changes in prices. However, there are a number of potential problems associated with the use of aggregate data in the estimation of the price elasticity of demand. Most important, aggregating over individuals and service types reduces variation in the data and can lead to aggregation biases.

A study by Rosett and Huang (1973) was among the first observational studies of the demand for health that used individual-level data. The 1960 Survey of Consumer Expenditure was used to analyze the effect of prices on health care demand. Using constructed measures of coinsurance, Rosett and Huang estimated that the price elasticity of demand was –0.35 when the out-of-pocket price for health care is 20 percent of the market price. At higher out-of-pocket prices, they found much greater sensitivity in medical expenditures (elasticities up to –1.5). The relatively large demand elasticities may be due in part to the way they constructed the coinsurance measures. The methodology used could lead to overestimates of price responsiveness (Zweifel and Manning, 2000).

Using data on insurance plans in the United States, Canada, and the United Kingdom, Phelps and Newhouse (1974) estimated price elasticities of demand for health care across coinsurance ranges. The price elasticity was estimated to be –0.12 when coinsurance rates ranged between 20 and 25 percent. When coinsurance rates decreased to between 15 and 20 percent, the elasticity was reduced to –0.07. Further, coinsurance rates ranging from 10 to 15 percent yielded price elasticity estimates of –0.04. These results indicate that low levels of cost-sharing will lead to relatively small changes in health care demand.

Wedig (1988) took a slightly different approach to the question and examined the connection between health status and price responsiveness of the demand for physician visits. Elasticities were estimated using data from the 1980 National Medical Care Utilization and Expenditure Survey. The results showed that people who perceived their health status to be fair or poor were less price responsive (–0.16) than those who reported their health to be good or excellent (–0.35).

Eichner (1998) used insurance claims data from one large employer to estimate the price elasticity of demand for health care. To do so, Eichner isolated the behavioral response to changes in price using variation in out-of-pocket cost within a plan with an annual deductible during a calendar year. The structure of these plans allowed the price of care to fall during the calendar year as people reached their deductible. He interpreted the difference in expenditures between those who have met their deductible and those who have not as a behavioral response to variation in the cost of medical care. The estimates of the price elasticity of the demand for health care varied between –0.75 and –0.62.

Starting in the early 1970s, many researchers began using the occurrence of natural experiments as an alternative estimation strategy. In 1972, Scitovsky and Snyder studied the effect of the implementation of cost-sharing requirements in the health plan offered to the faculty and staff (and their dependents) of Stanford University. A 25 percent coinsurance rate was implemented in April 1967. Changes in the use of health care services between 1966 and 1968 were analyzed to determine the effects of coinsurance on demand. The results indicated that the price elasticity of demand for physician visits was –0.14, showing that the demand for health is quite inelastic. Since Scitovsky and Snyder were able to use individual-level data, they explored some issues in greater detail than had been possible in the previous literature. Their results indicated that there is not much variation across socioeconomic and demographic groups in the demand response to changes in the price of health care. In a related study, Scitovsky and McCall (1977) found that reduced use of services caused by the institution of coinsurance is not transitory. Service use remained at the lower level at least through the four-year follow-up period.

During the same period of time, Beck (1974) studied the effect of co-payments on health care use in Saskatchewan, Canada. In 1968, the health plan provided by the province implemented a program requiring copayments of $1.50 for each doctor visit.[1] Beck analyzed a sample of over 40,000 individuals in 21,900 households selected at random. The findings indicated that the price elasticity of demand for health care services was –0.07. The fact that the elasticity estimate found in this study was somewhat lower than that reported thus far may be due to a change in physicians' practice patterns in Saskatchewan. If physicians responded to lower use by prescribing more intensive treatments for those who do use their services, the effect would tend to work in the opposite direction of the individual demand response and, thus, the estimate provided by Beck would

---

[1]The $1.50 copayment in 1968 dollars is equal to $14.48 in 2000 dollars. (These prices are measured in U.S. dollars.) At the time of the implementation of copayments, Canadian and U.S. dollars had equivalent value.

understate the true effect of prices on the demand for health care services.

A more recent study that was based on a natural experiment analyzed the effect of copayments on the demand for health care services for individuals insured through Group Health Cooperative of Puget Sound (GHC) (Cherkin et al., 1989). In July 1985, the plan began requiring copayments of $5 for each outpatient visit and $25 for each visit to the emergency room.[2] Cherkin et al. improved upon the analyses of the 1970s by including a comparison group, which did not receive the policy change. The evaluation of use patterns before and after the policy change yielded price elasticity of demand estimates of –0.04 for all visits. In a related study, Cherkin et al. (1990) found no difference in demand responses to price changes across income groups. The estimates from these studies are not directly comparable to those discussed previously. The GHC is a large staff model HMO in Seattle, Washington. The effect of prices on demand for health care services is likely to be different for different types of health plans. The management of care in HMOs increases the constraints on consumers and thus affects their use decisions.

In response to the relatively wide range of price elasticity estimates in the early health demand literature (from –0.07 in Beck, 1974, to –1.5 in Rosett and Huang, 1973), the government funded a social insurance experiment that was designed to answer a number of important questions surrounding the demand for health care. The RAND Health Insurance Experiment (HIE) (Newhouse et al., 1993) ran from 1974 to 1982 and randomized families in six sites into different insurance plans. The plans varied by level of cost-sharing, out-of-pocket maximum expenditure, and size of deductibles. Although the HIE was conducted approximately 20 years ago, the results of the related studies are still considered the "gold standard" for health demand elasticity estimates. The experimental design enables researchers to sidestep all of the selection and endogeneity problems associated with observational studies. The analysis of the HIE compares health care use across individuals in different insurance plans. It is interesting to note that use of health care services in the HIE was not affected

---

[2]The $5 copayment in 1985 dollars is equal to $11.88 in 2000 dollars. The $25 copayment for emergency room visits is equal to $59.39 in 2000 dollars.

by the out-of-pocket maximums. Consequently, for estimation purposes all insurance plans with the same coinsurance structure were considered the same. For coinsurance rates between 0 and 25 percent, the price elasticity of medical expenditures was found to be –0.17. Consistent with the patterns seen in observational studies, the demand for health care was found to be somewhat more price sensitive as the coinsurance rate increased. In the HIE, coinsurance rates between 25 and 95 percent yielded elasticity estimates of –0.22. The magnitude of the elasticities estimated from the HIE fall at the lower end of the range of previous estimates.

Cost-sharing in the HIE was found to significantly reduce per capita medical expenditures. Among those with free care (0 percent coinsurance), per capita expenditures were found to be 46 percent higher than among those with a 95 percent coinsurance rate. Furthermore, increased deductibles regardless of coinsurance rates were found to reduce health care use (Keeler and Rolph, 1988). The cost-sharing strategies worked to reduce use by reducing the number of treatment episodes and not by reducing intensity of treatment once an individual accessed the medical care system (Keeler and Rolph, 1983). The reductions in episodes were spread across situations both where medical treatment would be highly effective (an infection that can be treated with antibiotics) and where medical treatment would likely provide the fewest benefits (a flu caused by a virus) (Lohr et al., 1986). This result indicates that cost-sharing is an imprecise way to reduce less appropriate care.

Although the experimental results of the HIE are viewed as the gold standard, some issues of external validity have been raised. First, the study was geographically limited, as it was implemented in only six sites. Differences in health care use patterns have been observed across regions and, therefore, the HIE results may not be generalizable to the full population. The HIE sites, however, were chosen to include places that differed in important ways. Further, the results from the HIE are old. The health care industry has changed substantially since the experiment was implemented. Managed care has grown to be a significant portion of the health care plan options offered in most markets. Further, progress with medical technology and pharmaceuticals has pushed forward rapidly. It is difficult to say whether the HIE results can predict consumer behavior in a health care system that has changed significantly. Finally, it is not clear how the results from the HIE can be applied to a whole health care market. There were a few HIE participants in each study site (approximately 1,000 in each). As a result, any one physician might have only a few patients facing the new cost-sharing regimes and, thus, they did not feel the effects of reduced demand. It seems likely that if a cost-sharing plan was widely implemented and the demand for physician services fell, the behavior of suppliers might change.

Income Elasticity of Demand for Health Care

Although there is a wide literature on the income elasticity of demand, we have chosen to provide only a brief summary of the key findings. For the purposes of considering policy changes, income is an important variable, but it cannot be easily manipulated. The effects of changes in variables that the policymaker can control, such as coinsurance rates and deductibles, warrant greater analysis.

Theoretically, the effect of income on the demand for health care should be small, if not zero, under full insurance. If consumers have access to free care, changes in income should not affect their ability to obtain medical services. The empirical estimates in the literature are consistent with theory. Phelps (1992) calculated income elasticities based on results from an HIE study (Keeler et al., 1988). He found that the demand for health care was relatively insensitive to change in income. The calculations yielded elasticities of 0.2 or less. This can be interpreted to say that a 1 percent increase in income will lead to a 0.2 percent increase in the demand for health care. Results from a number of observational studies are consistent with the finding from data based on the HIE (for examples, see Taylor and Wilensky, 1983; Holmer, 1984).

Income elasticities based on cross-sectional data or on time series data covering a relatively short period hold the level of available medical technology constant. As real income in the population increases, the aggregate demand for new medical technologies and new treatment approaches rises as well and innovation accelerates. The technical change that occurs will alter the patterns of health care use. Income elasticities that are estimated from long time series data typically show much greater sensitivity of health care demand to changes in income. Feldstein (1971) used data from 1958 to 1967 to estimate an income elasticity of 0.5. Similarly, McLaughlin (1987) found an income elasticity of 0.7 using data from 1972 to 1982. A recent study by DiMatteo and DiMatteo (1998) used data from 10 provinces in Canada from 1965 through 1991 and found a similar income elasticity of 0.8. The larger elasticities from the time series studies reflect the incorporation of the effects of technical change.

In addition, one study evaluating the CHAMPUS Reform Initiative provides some evidence on the effect of income on the demand for health care among DoD beneficiaries. Hosek et al. (1993) found that increasing income reduces the probability of any military outpatient visits as well as the number of visits among users. Similarly, higher incomes were found to reduce the probability of any military inpatient visits. The negative correlation between income and use of military health services likely reflects the fact that higher-income military families are more likely to use nonmilitary health services.

Time Price Elasticity of Demand for Health Care

It is widely recognized that time prices are an important determinant of the demand for medical care, but there is very little empirical evidence regarding the sensitivity of health care demand to changes in time prices. One study, however, does speak directly to the time price elasticity of demand. Janssen (1992) used data from the National Health Interview Survey from the Netherlands Central Bureau of Statistics to estimate the demand for health, paying particular attention to the effect of time prices on demand. The time price associated with a doctor visit consists of two parts, the time spent and the value of the time. Janssen defined the time spent to include travel time, waiting time, and treatment time. The value of the time used to visit the doctor is defined in some cases by the individual's market wage and by employment status in others. The study found time price elasticities in the range of –0.09 to –0.14. These results suggest that a 1 percent increase in the time price of medical care will lead to approximately a 0.11 percent decrease in the probability of visiting a general practitioner. For all employment groups, the time price elasticity of demand is negative and small, suggesting that people are not very sensitive to changes in time prices. Although the estimates are clustered together, one of the highest time price elasticities was found for people who are employed full-time as managers or directors. This result makes sense, since such people would likely have high opportunity costs of time.

Time costs may be of particular importance within the context of the MHS, since much of the care is provided at MTFs where there is no monetary cost to the individual. Under these circumstances, time costs become particularly important in determining patterns of use. Many people who are eligible to receive care at MTFs choose to use other providers that require a copayment. If waiting times are longer in the MTF setting, this choice likely reflects the effects of time prices on the demand for health care services.

PRICE ELASTICITY OF DEMAND FOR SPECIFIC TYPES OF SERVICES

Health care is a widely heterogeneous product. One might expect the demand for different types of medical services to respond differently to changes in price. In this section, we summarize the health demand literature that speaks directly about the demand for specific types of health services. When considering specific types of services, there is greater opportunity to observe important relationships between goods. For example, one might argue that inpatient and outpatient services could serve as substitutes for one another. Similarly, lab services and inpatient stays might be expected to be complements. With this in mind, we will identify any cross-price elasticities that are contained in the literature. In the following sections, we first present estimates of inpatient and outpatient demand elasticities. Subsequently, elasticity estimates for preventive and acute care are discussed. Then, we discuss the elasticity of demand for prescription drugs. Finally, we review the literature on the elasticity of demand for mental health services. The estimates from the literature are summarized in Table 3.2.

Main Findings

Although the price elasticity of demand for medical care in general is relatively low, certain types of care are found to be somewhat more price sensitive. Preventive care and pharmacy benefits are among those medical services with larger price elasticities. The finding that

Table 3.2

Key Studies with Price Elasticity Estimates for Specific Medical Services

Study	Method	Data/Population	Price Measure	Quantity Measure	Elasticity Estimates
Inpatient vs. Outpatient Services					
Newhouse and Phelps, 1974	Observational	Center for Health Administration Studies Survey, 1963	Coinsurance rates	Inpatient: length of stay / Outpatient: no. of visits	Inpatient: −0.1 / Outpatient: −0.1
Newhouse and Phelps, 1976	Observational	Center for Health Administration Studies Survey, 1963	Coinsurance rates	Probability of use	Inpatient: −0.17 / Outpatient: −0.11
Newhouse et al., 1993	Experiment	RAND HIE	Coinsurance rates	Medical expenditures	Inpatient: −0.14 to −0.17 / Outpatient: −0.17 to −0.31
Preventive vs. Acute Care					
Newhouse et al., 1993	Experiment	RAND HIE	Coinsurance rates	Medical expenditures	Preventive: −0.17 to −0.43 / Acute: −0.17 to −0.32
Prescription Drugs					
O'Brien, 1989	Natural experiment	Prescription drug use in the United Kingdom	Copayments	No. of prescriptions	−0.33
Lavers, 1989	Natural experiment	Prescription drug use in the United Kingdom	Copayments	No. of prescriptions	−0.15 to −0.20
Harris et al., 1990	Natural experiment	Group Health Cooperative of Puget Sound	Copayments	No. of prescriptions	10.7% decrease after $1.50 copay initiated
Smith, 1993	Observational	National prescription drug card service data	Coinsurance rates	No. of prescriptions	−0.10

Table 3.2 (continued)

Study	Method	Data/Population	Price Measure	Quantity Measure	Elasticity Estimates
Hughes and McGuire, 1995	Natural experiment	Data on prescription drug use in the United Kingdom	Copayments	No. of prescriptions	−0.35
Newhouse et al., 1993	Experiment	RAND HIE	Coinsurance rates	Expenditures on prescriptions	−0.17
Mental Health Services					
Hankin et al., 1980	Natural experiment	Columbia Health Plan claims data	Coinsurance rates	No. of visits	−0.02
McGuire, 1981	Observational	Joint Information Service Survey of office-based psychiatrists	Out-of-pocket costs	No. of visits	−1.0
Wells et al., 1982	Experiment	RAND HIE	Coinsurance rates	Expenditures on mental health care	−0.17
Wallen et al., 1986	Natural experiment	United Mine Workers of America medical claims data	Coinsurance rates	No. of visits	All: −0.32 Men: −0.50 Women: −0.31
Frank, 1985	Observational	Aggregate state-level data, 1970–1978	Price of psychiatric services	Per capita visits to psychiatrists	−1.0 to −2.0
Simon et al., 1996	Observational or quasi-experiment	Claims data from a large HMO	Coinsurance rates	Probability of using mental health services	−0.17 to −0.28

the demand for preventive care is more price sensitive than the demand for other types of care is not surprising. The number of available substitutes for a product is a major determinant of demand elasticity. In the case of preventive care, a number of goods and services could possibly serve as substitutes. As a result, when the price of care increases consumers are able to substitute away from preventive care toward other goods and services that promote health, such as nutritional supplements and healthy foods. In addition, preventive medical services may be seen as more discretionary than necessary and, thus, may be put off when the price of such care increases. Further, the opportunity cost of obtaining preventive care is much higher than it is when the patient is sick, particularly if the illness keeps the individual out of work. It is also likely that, since the benefits of preventive care accrue in the long-term, they are heavily discounted. The difference in elasticities may also reflect the fact that preventive care and prescription drugs are typically not as well covered by insurance.

Inpatient Versus Outpatient Demand Elasticities

An early study by Newhouse and Phelps (1974) focused on estimating the price elasticity of demand using data from the 1963 Center for Health Administration Studies survey. Their estimates serve as a lower bound on the overall price elasticity as they considered only the effect of price on the quantity of services used, not the effect of price on the decision to use any services at all. For hospital inpatient stays, they found that the quantity of services, measured in terms of the length of the inpatient stay, was not very responsive to changes in price. The estimated price elasticity for inpatient services was found to be –0.1. The elasticity estimates for physician visits were quite similar. A 1 percent increase in the price of a physician visit would lead to a 0.06 percent reduction in the number of visits demanded. In a later study, Newhouse and Phelps (1976) improved upon their prior methodology by using a two-part demand model to explicitly measure the effects of price on both the use of any care and the quantity or intensity of care. Their results suggest that slightly more than half of the effect of the reduction in demand resulting from an increase in price is due to the reduction in the number of people who obtain any care. For inpatient stays, the price elasticity of demand for any care was –0.17 and the price elasticity of length of stay was

–0.06. In the case of outpatient visits, the price elasticity of any use was –0.11 and the elasticity of demand for visits was –0.08. The New-house and Phelps studies (1974, 1976) did not address the issue of the cross-price elasticity between inpatient and outpatient care.

The most comprehensive results on the effect of price on the de-mand for inpatient and outpatient services are based on data from the HIE. Newhouse et al. (1993) provided estimates of elasticity by type of service received. With coinsurance rates in the range of 0 to 25 percent the price elasticity of demand for both outpatient and inpatient services was found to be –0.17. When coinsurance rates increased to 25 to 95 percent, however, the demand for outpatient services was found to be more price sensitive than the demand for hospital stays (–0.31 and –0.14, respectively). In a related study, Lei-bowitz et al. (1985) compared demand responsiveness across age groups. They found that children's and adult's demand for outpa-tient services is equally responsive to price changes. For inpatient services, however, price changes have no effect on the quantity of services demanded for children.

The design of the HIE allowed researchers to address the question of the cross-price elasticity between inpatient and outpatient services. One health plan variation included in the HIE required coinsurance payments for outpatient services but not for inpatient hospital stays. An analysis by Manning et al. (1987) indicated that there was no substitution between inpatient and outpatient services. In fact, they found just the opposite. Inpatient use was actually somewhat higher in the group that had to pay coinsurance for their stays. Although the difference is not statistically significant, it could suggest that inpa-tient and outpatient services are actually complements in use.

The movement toward managed care in the MHS provides a natural experiment to analyze the effect of price changes on use among DoD beneficiaries. Goldman (1995) studied the CHAMPUS Reform Initia-tive (CRI) and found differences in the use response between inpa-tient and outpatient care. The CRI, a pilot test for TRICARE, covered 850,000 beneficiaries in California and Hawaii. The CRI offered MHS beneficiaries the choice of enrolling in an HMO or in a PPO. Gold-man used a sophisticated statistical model to address self-selection issues associated with the choice of enrolling in the HMO or PPO. The results from this analysis showed that the demand for outpatient care was 16 percent higher in the HMO than in the baseline fee-for-service (FFS) plan. The HMO option involved lower out-of-pocket costs for civilian visits; however, MTF care remained free in all plans. Most of this increase under the HMO can be attributed to a greater probability of any use rather than an increase in the number of visits per person. It is interesting to note that there does not appear to be any difference in outpatient use between the PPO and FFS. The aggressive use reviews in the HMO and PPO appear to have decreased inpatient days relative to FFS. However, the CRI did not appear to deter inpatient admissions.

Preventive Care Versus Acute Care Demand Elasticities

The literature suggests that the demand for preventive care, or well care, is somewhat more responsive to price than either acute or chronic care. Newhouse et al. (1993) used data from the HIE to estimate demand elasticities for each of these categories of care. At lower levels of coinsurance (0 to 25 percent), the price elasticity of demand for these service types is quite similar and centers on –0.17. When coinsurance rates are between 25 and 95 percent, however, differences in the elasticities of demand are found. The demand for preventive care is found to be the most price sensitive, with an elasticity of –0.43. The demand elasticities for acute and chronic are –0.32 and –0.23, respectively.

Cherkin et al. (1990) provided some insight into the effect of price on the demand for preventive care based on data from a natural experiment. They found that after the imposition of $5 copayments for outpatient visits, preventive outpatient visits fell by 14 percent whereas the number of outpatient visits fell by only 11 percent.[3] Although the difference is relatively small, the results from Newhouse et al. (1993) suggest that as the level of cost-sharing (in this case the copayment) increases, the demand responsiveness increases as well.

------

[3]The $5 copayment in 1983 dollars is equal to $11.88 in 2000 dollars.

Price Elasticity of Demand for Prescription Drugs

The demand for prescription drugs is another category of medical services that has been analyzed in the literature. In 1983, Group Health Associates implemented a cost-sharing prescription drug plan in Washington state. Harris et al. (1990) analyzed the effect of a $1.50 copayment on demand and found a 10.7 percent decrease in the number of prescriptions. A further increase in the copayment from $1.50 per prescription to $5 per prescription reduced prescriptions by an additional 10.6 percent.[4] Using the numbers reported, we calculate the own-price elasticity of demand for prescription drugs to be between –0.05 and –0.08, indicating inelastic demand.

In a similar study, Smith (1993) analyzed the effect of an increase in prescription drug copayments from $2 to $5 on prescription drug use for a set of employer groups covered by one national managed care company.[5] This study found a price elasticity of demand for pharmaceuticals equal to –0.10. This elasticity can be interpreted as a 1 percent increase in the price of prescription drugs leads to a 0.1 percent decrease in the number of prescription claims. Smith noted, however, that although the number of prescriptions fell in response to the price increase, there was an offsetting increase in the ingredient costs per prescription. This suggests that physicians compensated for the increased price to consumers by prescribing larger amounts per prescription. In addition, this study found that the increase in drug copayments led to a 10 percent decrease in employer costs per person and an increase in employee costs.

A number of studies of the price elasticity of demand for prescription drugs use data from the United Kingdom. Copayments for prescriptions were implemented beginning in 1968. O'Brien (1989) took advantage of the natural experiment and estimated a price elasticity of –0.33. Further, the study found a positive cross-price elasticity of 0.17 between prescription and over-the-counter drugs. A positive cross-price elasticity indicates that two goods are substitutes in use. Hughes and McGuire (1995) used a more complicated estimation

---

[4]The $1.50 and $5 prescription drug copayments are equal to approximately $4 and $12, respectively, in 2000 dollars.

[5]The increase in copayments from $2 to $5 per prescription in 1989 dollars is equal to an increase from $3.62 to $9.06 in 2000 dollars.

model and found similar results using data from the United Kingdom. Lavers (1989), using data from the United Kingdom for the years 1971 through 1982, found prescription drug elasticities that were somewhat lower. His results suggest that a 1 percent increase in price will lead to a reduction in the number of prescriptions somewhere in the range of 0.15 to 0.20 percent.

Results from the HIE indicate that prescription drug use is responsive to cost-sharing. The per person prescription expenditure in the free care plan was nearly two times higher than the per person expenditure in the plan with a 95 percent coinsurance requirement ($82 and $46, respectively) (Newhouse et al., 1993). The reduction in drug expenditures, however, can be attributed in large part to the differences in visit rates between the two plans. The prescription drug cost per visit was found to be quite similar across plans. Since there was no independent variation in the prescription drug coinsurance (they were the same as the visit coinsurance rates), it is difficult to isolate the effect of price on prescription drug demand from the HIE data. The study concluded that the elasticity of demand for prescription drugs is similar to the elasticity of demand for health care in general.

Although there are numerous studies on the elasticity of demand for prescription drugs, very few focus on the elderly population (Grootendorst et al., 1997). This group should be of particular interest because they typically have higher medical care needs and costs and their population is growing rapidly. A study undertaken in Canada by Grootendorst et al. (1997) sought to fill this gap in the literature. They used data from the Ontario Health Survey to study the effect of first-dollar prescription drug coverage on drug use by seniors. At age 65, individuals in Ontario become eligible for the Ontario Drug Benefit Plan. The study compared prescription drug use before and after the statutory date of eligibility. The study found an upward shift in prescription drug use by seniors at age 65 even after controlling for health status and other demographic factors. In addition, the results suggest that the increase in prescription drug use is driven by increases in drug volume among users rather than by increases in the probability of any use. Consistent with this result is the finding that persons with poorer reported health status are more likely to increase prescription drug use with first-dollar coverage.

Price Elasticity of Demand for Mental Health Services

Studying the demand for mental health care can be more complicated than studying demand for other specific types of medical care. Mental health insurance benefits have historically been much more limited than benefits for general medical care. Recent parity laws, however, have changed the market for specialty mental health services by requiring equal coverage of mental health and general medical care. As the parity laws have only recently been implemented, their effect on the use of mental health services is not yet fully understood. An additional aspect making the demand for mental health care more difficult to measure is that people often feel a stigma associated with mental health care. Because of this, people may not file insurance claims for mental health treatment if their insurance is through their employer. Consequently, a larger portion of mental health care may be self-paid and will not be reflected in the claims databases that are often used to estimate the medical care demand equations. In addition, the perceived stigma may also affect self-reported use of mental health services in surveys.

Much of the evidence on the elasticity of demand for mental health care comes from natural experiments. In these studies, the variation in the price of services is generated by the introduction of or changes in the level of copayments. In 1978 the Columbia Health Plan in Maryland increased copayments from $2 to $10 per mental health visit.[6] Hankin et al. (1980) showed that the increase in price led to a decrease in the number of mental health visits per 1,000 population covered from 414.4 to 404.7. These results suggest an elasticity of demand equal to –0.02 for outpatient mental health services. Hankin et al. noted that although this elasticity estimate is quite low, over the same time period the Columbia Health Plan increased access to mental health services by increasing treatment staff. The decrease in waiting periods and appointment delays likely had an offsetting effect on use and, thus, the price elasticity estimate is biased downward.

In 1978, the United Mine Workers of America entered into a new agreement with their employers regarding health benefits provisions.

---

[6]The increase in copayments from $2 to $10 in 1978 dollars is equal to an increase from $8.72 to $43.58 in 2000 dollars.

The new agreement required copayments for all physician visits. This natural experiment was studied by Roddy et al. (1986). The introduction of $5 copayments was found to reduce the number of mental health visits per 1,000 enrollees from 110.15 to 60.07.[7] The elasticity of demand for mental health services was found to be –0.32, suggesting that a 1 percent increase in price leads to a 0.32 percent decrease in the demand for outpatient mental health visits. This finding indicates that the demand for mental health services is inelastic but is at least as large as the price elasticity of demand for general medical care. In a related article, Wallen et al. (1986) studied the differential effect of the copayments on the use of mental health services between men and women. They found that men are more sensitive than women to changes in the price of a mental health visit. The elasticities are estimated to be –0.50 and –0.31, respectively.

In two related articles, Simon et al. (1994, 1996) studied the effect of the institution of and subsequent increase in the required copayments for mental health services within an HMO. They found a reduction of 33 percent (56 percent) in the probability of any mental health service use when $20 ($30) copayments were introduced.[8] These findings produce elasticity of demand estimates ranging from –0.17 to –0.28. These elasticities are based on the probability of any use and are thus interpreted somewhat differently from the other estimates presented in this section. These elasticity estimates suggest that a 1 percent increase in the price of mental health services will lead to a 0.17 to 0.28 percent decrease in the rate of any mental health service use among the enrollee population. Simon et al. found very little effect from the introduction of the $20 copayment on the visit rate among service users.

Studies based on observational data have found elasticities that are quite a bit larger than those found in the studies based on natural experiments. McGuire (1981) used data from the Joint Information Service Survey of office-based psychiatrists in 1973. He concluded that the elasticity of demand for psychotherapy is –1.0 or greater. The study, however, is limited by the adequacy of the data. Because

---

[7]The $5 copayment in 1978 dollars is equal to $21.79 in 2000 dollars.

[8]The $20 and $30 copayments in 1991 dollars are equal to $30.12 and $45.18, respectively, in 2000 dollars.

of the structure of the sample, only those in treatment were included and heavy users of mental health services were overrepresented. This estimate of the price elasticity found by McGuire is relatively large, but it is not outside the range of other observational estimates. Frank (1985) used state-level data from 1970 to 1978 and found elasticity estimates in the range of –1.0 to –2.0.

The RAND HIE also looked at the effect of copayments on mental health service use. Wells et al. (1982) concluded that the demand for ambulatory mental health care and ambulatory medical care exhibit similar responses to variations in price generated by copayments.

THE ELASTICITY OF DEMAND FOR HEALTH INSURANCE

Apart from studies on the responsiveness of the demand for health care to price and income, there is growing attention to the responsiveness of demand for different health plans to changes in the price of insurance. This literature is of particular importance when considering the demand for health care services provided by a particular health plan. Any change in the out-of-pocket costs of services or premium costs will have an effect on the number of plan enrollees and, thus, on the demand for health care services paid for by that plan. In this section, we review studies of the effects of changes in health insurance plans on the demand for health insurance. We focus on the choice between different health plans and do not discuss studies on the decision whether to purchase any insurance at all.[9] First, we present the main findings in the literature. Then, we discuss the studies in more detail (see Table 3.3).

Main Findings

According to Royalty and Solomon (1998), "there is no definitely established range of price elasticities [of health plan choice] in the literature." Econometric studies of health care plan choice vary dramatically, not only in their price elasticity estimates but also in the data sources, econometric methods, and experimental design. For

---

[9]For a recent study on the decision to purchase insurance, including a literature review, see Marquis and Long (1995).

Table 3.3

Key Studies on the Elasticity of Demand for Health Insurance

Study	Methodology	Population Under Study	Elasticity Definition	Price Elasticity
Cutler and Reber, 1996	Natural experiment	10,000 Harvard University employees	Change in PPO enrollment resulting from a 1 percent increase in out-of-pocket premium	−0.3 to −0.6
Marquis and Phelps, 1987	Experiment	Families in RAND Health Insurance Experiment	Change in enrollment of full supplementary insurance resulting from a 1 percent increase in premium	−0.6
Short and Taylor, 1989	Observational study	Nationally representative cross-section dataset from National Medical Care Expenditure Survey (NMCES), 1977	1) Change in probability of enrollment in "high option" FFS relative to "low option" FFS from a 1 percent increase in net premium 2) Change in probability of enrollment in HMO relative to FFS plan from 1 percent increase in net premium	−0.14 −0.05
Royalty and Solomon, 1998	Observational study	Panel data of Stanford University Emp.	Change in percentage enrolled resulting from a 1 percent increase in premiums	−1.0 to −1.8 (logit) −3.7 to −6.2 (fixed effects)
Barringer and Mitchell, 1994	Observational study	Payroll benefits from single company in United States	Changes in the fraction of people choosing a plan relative to a 1 percent increase in the premium	−0.1 to −0.2
Hosek et al., 1995	Observational study	Military personnel	Change in probability of choosing the civilian plan relative to a 1 percent increase in premium	−0.6
Feldman, et al., 1989	Natural experiment	20 firms in Minneapolis	Change in enrollment in a plan with 50 percent of the overall market due to a 1 percent increase in the premium	−0.15 to −0.53

example, the articles reviewed in this report use datasets of individual employees and their health plan choices in various professional and demographic settings, such as a single university, 20 firms within one city, a single company with four plants across the United States, and a national cross-section, among others. Some of these are panel datasets, and others are purely cross-sectional. Studies on the demand for health insurance tend to be either observational (among others, Merrill, Jackson, and Reuter, 1985) or natural experiments (among others, Cutler and Reber, 1996). However, as an offspring of the RAND Health Insurance Experiment, one study examines the demand for supplementary insurance based on a randomized experiment (Marquis and Phelps, 1987).

When estimating price elasticity, the possibility of adverse selection needs to be considered if the health of plan enrollees is a concern. However, if we are simply interested in the effects of price changes on the market share for each plan, then the presence of adverse selection is not important. Adverse selection occurs when people with relatively high expected expenditures on health care choose a relatively generous insurance plan. When these anticipations appear to be accurate and actually realized, the more generous insurance plan may have to increase premiums, resulting in further selection between people with different anticipated health expenditures. Adverse selection is likely to be manifested in differential enrollment over a period of years. Therefore, the long-run response to a change in (relative) premiums will be larger than the short-run response, as we will see in the next subsection.

It is difficult to obtain health insurance price elasticity estimates from cross-sectional plan choice studies, because there is typically very little variation in premiums across plans and any observed variation is correlated with quality of or access to care. Therefore, results from studies based solely on cross-sectional data should be interpreted carefully.

Studies on the Price Elasticity of Demand for Different Health Plans

Cutler and Reber (1996) investigated enrollment decisions when the relative prices of an HMO and a PPO health plan changed. Harvard

University employees could choose between two plans: a low-cost HMO plan that restricts choice of providers and provider income and a high-cost PPO plan with fewer restrictions on choice and more generous provider reimbursement. In 1995, Harvard University moved from a system of subsidizing generous insurance to a system of paying a fixed contribution independent of plan choice (some 80 percent). The price elasticity, defined as the percentage change in PPO enrollment resulting from a 1 percent change in the out-of-pocket premium, was estimated to be –0.3 in the first year and –0.6 in the second year. The policy change also induced substantial adverse selection. As a result, the long-run demand response was three times higher, and the market for more generous insurance appears to have been eliminated entirely.

In a similar study, Buchmueller and Feldstein (1997) reported results from a natural experiment where the University of California (UC) system made changes to employee health insurance benefits that resulted in increased premiums for many employees. The study found that consumers were quite sensitive to changes in out-of-pocket premiums and were willing to switch health plans in response to small premium changes. More specifically, they estimated that 26 percent of enrollees would switch to another plan when premiums rose by $10 per month. As a comparison, only 5 percent of individuals whose premium remained constant switched to a different plan. It is likely that the estimates from this study serve as an upper bound. The UC system provided standardized benefits across the different plans. As a result, the primary differences between plans were out-of-pocket premiums and the list of approved providers. This factor makes the comparison across plans relatively straightforward for consumers. In less-controlled situations where the services covered vary between plans, the consumer's decision to change health plans is more complex as the plans may not be close substitutes.

Royalty and Solomon (1998) used a panel dataset from the Stanford University Benefits Office to estimate price elasticities for health insurance plan choices. The price variation that identified the elasticity estimates came from differences in premiums across plan choices. The price elasticity calculations ranged from –1.0 to –1.8 in their simple logit estimations and –3.7 to –6.2 in their fixed effects model. Their goal was to investigate the extent of price responsiveness by employees in a managed competition market and how "transition costs" depress this price elasticity. Such transition costs include doctor-patient relationships and other characteristics that are difficult to quantify. The authors found a "striking, although not always statistically significant, difference in the estimated price elasticities by group that go in the direction predicted if there are greater costs in switching health plans for those who are older, sicker, or who have worked at Stanford longer." Thus, younger and healthier employees were more price sensitive.

Feldman et al. (1989) determined the price elasticity of health plan choice using data from a survey of employees in 20 Minneapolis firms conducted in 1984. The firms employed 7.2 percent of the Twin Cities workforce. The key findings were that (1) employees were less likely to choose health plans with higher monthly out-of-pocket premiums, (2) employees prefered health plans that offered preventive coverage, and (3) fee-for-service plans tended to be preferred over IPAs and HMOs (other things equal), but this effect diminished as the number of years the plan was offered increased. One difficulty in interpreting the results of this study is that the estimated own-price elasticity depends on both the market share of the health plan itself and the share of alternatives within the same nest. According to Royalty and Solomon (1998), the Feldman et al. results imply that a health plan with 50 percent of overall market has price elasticities ranging from –0.53 to –0.15, depending on the share of the plan within its nest. Plans with very small enrollments thus have even larger elasticities, and very large plans have elasticities close to zero. Royalty and Solomon have criticized the study for not including interactions of income with plan attributes, potentially biasing price elasticities.

Short and Taylor (1989) use data from the 1977 National Medical Care Expenditure Survey (NMCES) to estimate two elasticities—one for the choice between two FFS plans and one for the choice between a FFS and an HMO. The price elasticity of the probability of enrolling in the "high option" FFS relative to the "low option" FFS based on premium differences was –0.14. The price elasticity of enrolling in an HMO relative to FFS was –0.05.

Barringer and Mitchell (1994) estimated the effect of changes in premiums and deductibles on employees' preferences for four types of health care plans. The data came from employee payroll benefit records from a single company with four plants across the United States. The authors found that increasing the traditional FFS premium by 10 percent reduced the fraction choosing the plan by 4 to 9 percent. A 10 percent rise in the deductible of the traditional FFS led to a change in market share of 0 to 1 percent. Doubling the traditional FFS deductible implied a market share decline of 3 to 4 percent. A 10 percent increase in salary corresponded to a 1 to 2 percent increase in the traditional FFS. The price elasticities with respect to changes in premium were in the range of –0.1 to –0.2.

In a study of the demand for health care in the military, Hosek et al. (1995) examined the choice of enrollment in a civilian plan versus a military health plan for active duty and retired families. The authors calculated a price elasticity of demand for health plan choice of –0.6. This finding indicates that a 1 percent increase in the premium level for the civilian plan leads to a 0.6 percent decrease in the probability of choosing this plan. The magnitude of this elasticity is quite similar to other estimates from the literature that are based on the civilian population.

The Income Elasticity of Demand for Different Health Plans

Family income likely has an effect on the choice between different health plans. A study of the CHAMPUS Reform Initiative provides some evidence of this effect and estimates of the income elasticity of demand for health plan choice. Hosek et al. (1993) found that a 10 percent increase in household income decreased the probability that a family would enroll in CHAMPUS Prime (the HMO choice) by 0.24 percentage points. Using the information provided in that report, we calculate an income elasticity of demand for enrollment in CHAMPUS Prime as –0.27. This suggests that a 1 percent increase in income will reduce the probability of enrollment in the HMO option by 0.27 percent.

The Price Elasticity of Demand for Supplementary Insurance

As part of the RAND Health Insurance Experiment, Marquis and Phelps (1987) estimated the demand elasticity for supplementary insurance. Each family was presented a hypothetical offer to supplement its insurance coverage by reducing the amount of its annual maximum dollar expenditure (MDE), beyond which the plan paid 100 percent. There were three options: a one-third reduction in the MDE, a two-thirds reduction, or full coverage. The authors estimated the probability that a family would express interest in the insurance product.

The "loading fee," which is equal to the expected payout from the insurance plan (defined as the difference between the price and the benefits) divided by the benefits,[10] was used as a measure of the price of supplementary insurance. The expected payout was based on expected expenditures on health care and the amount of coverage. Generally speaking, when the loading fee (i.e., the price measure) is low, it is attractive to buy insurance. The results showed that an increase in the loading fee decreases the interest in all offered supplementary insurance options and that demand for supplementation could be sufficiently large to diminish responses to copayment changes. Clearly, if people supplement away any copayments, the use-reducing effects of cost-sharing may be affected negatively. The estimate of the price elasticity of the demand for full supplementary insurance is –0.6.

------

[10]Thus: loading fee = (price–benefits)/benefits

CONSIDERING THE POTENTIAL EFFECTS OF CURRENT AND PROPOSED CHANGES IN TRICARE BENEFITS

The FY 2001 National Defense Authorization Act was signed into law by President Clinton on October 30, 2000. Although the act contains numerous changes, four new TRICARE initiatives will have important effects on uniformed services retirees and their spouses.

- Expanding pharmacy benefits for seniors to include access to MTF pharmacies, the National Mail Order Pharmacy Program (NMOP), and retail pharmacies,

- Making TRICARE a second payer to Medicare (TRICARE for Life),

- Eliminating coinsurance payments under TRICARE Prime for dependents of active duty personnel, and

- Expanding TRICARE Prime Remote benefits to active duty family members and nonuniformed service members.

In this final chapter, we briefly describe how the demand literature applies to these changes.

EXPANSION OF PHARMACY BENEFITS

The expansion of pharmacy benefits for Medicare-eligible MHS beneficiaries will likely lead to increases in the demand for prescription drugs provided through the TRICARE program. The new prescription coverage requires no enrollment fee, but participants will be required to make modest copayments for the prescriptions they receive. If individuals choose to obtain prescriptions outside the network, they will be required to pay a deductible and somewhat higher copayments per prescription.

Previously, some Medicare-eligible beneficiaries obtained prescriptions at MTF pharmacies and others paid for prescriptions themselves or through other insurance. Demand for prescriptions provided through TRICARE will increase because Medicare-eligible beneficiaries who previously paid themselves will now finance their prescriptions through TRICARE and some who used other insurance will switch to TRICARE.[1] For example, the CBO (2000) estimates that approximately 360,000 additional people will use the NMOP benefit. Many of these seniors will be able to fill their prescriptions at lower out-of-pocket prices and so they will purchase greater numbers of prescriptions. The results from the civilian literature suggest that the price elasticity of demand for prescription drugs is in the range of –0.3. This means that when the price of prescriptions falls by 1 percent the demand for prescriptions will increase by 0.3 percent. This increase in demand will occur in part because consumers will substitute away from using over-the-counter drugs that are now relatively more expensive toward prescription drugs. The results from the literature indicate that with a 1 percent reduction in the price of prescription drugs, the demand for over-the-counter drugs will fall by 0.17 percent.

TRICARE FOR LIFE

The second major change to the MHS makes TRICARE the second payer to Medicare. Under the new law, enrollment in Medicare Part B is required for participation in the second payer plan, unless the individual was Medicare eligible before April 1, 2001. Having TRICARE as a second payer will substitute for the Medigap insurance that most senior military beneficiaries have and will eliminate most of their out-of-pocket health care costs. This reduction in the effective price can be expected to lead to greater demand for health care services. TRICARE will pay most of the costs not paid by Medicare at prior demand levels, replacing Medigap and self-financing. It will

---

[1]Some beneficiaries may switch from MTF pharmacies to civilian pharmacies, but the change in demand from this group should be small.

also finance a share of any demand increase resulting from lower patient cost-sharing.

Although most of the economic studies that we have summarized focus on the nonelderly adult population, there is evidence to suggest that seniors do respond to price decreases with increases in use. As evidence, numerous studies have shown that, among Medicare recipients, use of health care services is higher for those who have Medigap supplemental insurance (for examples, see Link et al., 1980; Christensen et al., 1987; McCall et al., 1991; Cartwright et al., 1992). These studies are particularly relevant because, as we indicated above, the new law makes TRICARE a substitute for other Medigap policies. Unfortunately, none of these studies provide price-elasticity estimates. Therefore, we cannot directly compare the level of price sensitivity between the elderly and nonelderly adult populations. However, we expect that the estimates from the literature may serve as a lower bound for the elasticity of demand for health care and health insurance among the elderly. Senior citizens are typically expected to have more elastic demands for goods and services. This is due in part to the fact that health expenditures make up a larger portion of the total budget for senior citizens than for other adults.

ELIMINATION OF COPAYMENTS IN TRICARE PRIME

In the case of TRICARE Prime, the elimination of copayments for civilian care provided to active duty dependents is likely to have two effects on the demand for MHS-paid medical services. First, the economic literature predicts that reductions in copayments will increase the number of current enrollees who access any care, particularly among those who rely on civilian providers. The literature also indicates, however, that the price elasticity of demand for health care is relatively low at low levels of cost-sharing (see Newhouse et al., 1993). The current copayments for active duty dependents are relatively low, ranging from $6 to $12 per visit. Therefore, the effect on use of eliminating these copayments may be relatively small. Further, TRICARE Prime enrollees will now face the same price for services obtained through civilian doctors or through MTFs. To the extent that some people had previously chosen to use MTF services because of the lower cost, the elimination of copayments for civilian care could lead to some substitution from MTF care to civilian care.

Although this may not lead to an increase in the number of total physician visits among current enrollees, the shift from one type of provider to another could have cost implications for the MHS.

The second effect of the elimination of copayments in TRICARE Prime is that some beneficiaries may choose to switch between TRI-CARE plans. The lower out-of-pocket costs for civilian care may make the Prime option more attractive to families that had previously chosen the Extra or Standard TRICARE options.[2] The literature on the elasticity of health care plan choice suggests that some switching between plans does occur in response to changes in plan characteristics. The magnitude of such effects, however, has not been well established.

TRICARE PRIME REMOTE

The expansion of the TRICARE Prime Remote benefits to dependents of active duty personnel and uniformed service personnel (i.e., personnel from the Public Health Service, the Coast Guard, and the National Oceanic and Atmospheric Administration) will likely increase the demand for health care services paid through the TRICARE program. Most of the affected beneficiaries must now use TRICARE Standard, which imposes significant copayments. The reduction in out-of-pocket costs may increase the demand for care, especially if Prime cost-control mechanisms are less effective for this dispersed population than they are for more concentrated populations.

---

[2]Families eligible for health insurance through the spouse's employer would be expected to find TRICARE relatively more attractive. However, this effect will be negligible as very few active duty families now use other insurance.

Barringer, M. W., and O. S. Mitchell (1994), "Worker's preferences among company-provided health insurance plans," *Industrial and Labor Relations Review* 48(1):141–152.

Beck, R. G. (1974), "The effects of copayment on the poor," *Journal of Human Resources* 9:129–142.

Buchmueller, T. C., and P. J. Feldstein (1997), "The effect of price on switching among health plans," *Journal of Health Economics* 16(2):231–247.

Cartwright, W. S., T.-W. Hu, and L.-F. Huang (1992), "Impact of varying Medigap insurance coverage on the use of medical services of the elderly," *Applied Economics* 24:529–539.

Cherkin, D. C., L. Grothaus, and E. H. Wagner (1989), "The effect of office visit copayments on preventive care services in an HMO," *Inquiry* 27(1):24–38.

Cherkin, D. C., L. Grothaus, and E. H. Wagner (1990), "The effect of office visit copayments on utilization in a health maintenance organization," *Medical Care* 27(11):1036–1045.

Christensen, S., S. H. Long, and J. Rodgers (1987), "Acute health care costs for the aged Medicare population: Overview and policy options," *Milbank Quarterly* 65(3):397–425.

Congressional Budget Office (CBO) (1988), *Reforming the Military Health Care System*, Washington, D.C.

Congressional Budget Office (May 1, 2000), Congressional Budget Office Cost Estimate; S.2087 Military Health Care Improvements Act of 2000, as introduced February 23, 2000, available at http://www.cbo.gov/showdoc.cfm?index=2011&sequence=0&from=6.

Cook, T. D., and D. T. Campbell (1979), *Quasi-Experimentation: Design and Analysis Issues for Field Settings,* Rand McNally College Publishing Company, Chicago, Illinois.

Cutler, D. M., and S. Reber (1996), "Paying for health insurance: The tradeoff between competition and adverse selection," Working Paper, No. 5796, National Bureau of Economic Research, New York.

Cutler, D. M., and R. J. Zeckhauser (1999), "The anatomy of health insurance," Working Paper, No. 7176, National Bureau of Economic Research, New York.

DiMatteo, L., and R. DiMatteo (1998), "Evidence on the determinants of Canadian provincial government health expenditures: 1965–1991," *Journal of Health Economics* 17:211–228.

Eichner, M. J. (1998), "The demand for medical care: What people pay does matter," *American Economic Review* 88(2):117–121, May.

Feldman, R., et al. (1989), "The demand for employment-based health insurance plans," *Journal of Human Resources* 24(1):115–142.

Feldstein, M. S. (1971), "Hospital cost inflation: A study of nonprofit price dynamics," *American Economic Review* 60:853–872.

Feldstein, M. S. (1973), "The welfare loss of excessive health insurance," *Journal of Political Economy* 81(1):251–280.

Frank, R. G. (1985), "Pricing and location of physician services in mental health," *Economic Inquiry* 23:115–133.

Fuchs, V. R., and M. J. Kramer (1972), *Determinants of expenditures for physicians' services in the United States, 1948–1968,* Occasional Paper No. 117, National Bureau of Economic Research, New York.

General Accounting Office (GAO) (2000), "Observations on proposed benefit expansion and overcoming TRICARE obstacles," Statement of Stephen P. Backhus, Director, Veterans' Affairs and Military Health Care Issues GAO/T-HEHS/NSIAD-00-129.

Getzen, T. E. (2000), "Health care is an individual necessity and a national luxury: Applying multilevel decision models to the analysis of health care expenditures," *Journal of Health Economics* 19:259–270.

Goldman, D. P. (1995), "Managed care as a public cost-containment mechanism," *RAND Journal of Economics* 26(2):277–295.

Goldman, D. P., et al. (1995), "The effects of benefit design and managed care on health care costs," *Journal of Health Economics* 14:401–418.

Grootendorst, P. V., et al. (1997), "On becoming 65 in Ontario: Effects of drug plan eligibility on use of prescription medicines," *Medical Care* 35(4):386–398.

Grossman, M. (1972), "On the concept of health capital and demand for health," *Journal of Political Economy* 80(2):223–255.

Hankin, J. R., D. M. Steinwachs, and E. Charmain (1980), "The impact of a copayment increase for ambulatory psychiatric care," *Medical Care* 18(8):807–815.

Harris, B. L., A. Stergachis, and L. D. Ried (1990), "The effect of drug copayments on utilization and cost of pharmaceuticals in a health maintenance organization," *Medical Care* 28(10):907–917.

Holmer, M. (1984), "Tax policy and the demand for health insurance," *Journal of Health Economics* 3:203–221.

Hosek, S. D., et al. (1993), *Evaluation of the CHAMPUS Reform Initiative: Volume 3, Health Care Utilization and Costs*, RAND R-4244/3-HA, Santa Monica, California.

Hosek, S. D., B. W. Bennet, et al. (1995), *The Demand for Military Health Care: Supporting Research for a Comprehensive Study of the Military Health-Care System*, RAND MR-407-1-OSD, Santa Monica, California.

Hughes, D., and A. McGuire (1995), "Patient charges and the utilization of NHS prescription medicines," *Health Economics* 4(3):213–220.

Janssen, R. (1992), "Time prices and the demand for GP services," *Social Sciences and Medicine* 34(7):725–733.

Keeler, E. B., and J. E. Rolph (1983), "How cost sharing reduced medical spending of participants in the health insurance experiment," *Journal of the American Medical Association* 249(16):2220–2227.

Keeler, E. B., and J. E. Rolph (1988), "The demand for episodes of treatment in the health insurance experiment," *Journal of Health Economics* 7(4):337–367.

Keeler, E. B., J. L. Buchanan, J. E. Rolph, et al. (1988), *The Demand for Episodes of Treatment in the Health Insurance Experiment*, RAND R-3454-HHS, Santa Monica, California.

Lavers, R. (1989), "Prescription charges, the demand for prescriptions and morbidity," *Applied Economics* 21:1043–1052.

Leibowitz, A., W. G. Manning, et al. (1985), "The effect of cost sharing on the use of medical services of children: Interim results from a randomized controlled trial," *Pediatrics* 75(5):942–951.

Levy, R. A., R. Miller, and P. Branman (2000), *The DOD Health Care Benefit: How Does It Compare to FEHBP and Other Plans?* Center for Naval Analyses, Research Memorandum D0001316.A1, Washington, D.C., May.

Link, C. R., S. H. Long, and R. F. Settle (1980), "Cost sharing, supplementary insurance, and health services utilization among the Medicare elderly," *Health Care Financing Review* 2(2):25–31.

Lohr, K. N., R. H. Brook, C. J. Kamberg, et al. (1986), "Effect of cost sharing on use of medically effective and less effective care," *Medical Care* 24(9 Suppl):S31–S38.

Manning, W. G., J. P. Newhouse, N. Duan, et al. (1987), "Health insurance and the demand for medical care: Evidence from a randomized experiment," *American Economic Review* 77(3):251–277.

Manning, W. G., J. P. Newhouse, N. Duan, et al. (1988), *Health insurance and the demand for medical care: Evidence from a randomized experiment*, RAND R-3476-HHS, Santa Monica, California.

Marquis, M. S., and S. H. Long (1995), "Worker demand for health insurance in the non-group market," *Journal of Health Economics* 14:47–63.

Marquis, M. S., and C. E. Phelps (1987), "Price elasticity and adverse selection in the demand for supplementary health insurance," *Economic Inquiry* 25(2):299–313.

McCall, N., T. Rice, J. Boismier, et al. (1991), "Private health insurance and medical care utilization: Evidence from the Medicare population," *Inquiry* 28(3):276–287.

McGuire, T. (1981), *Financing Psychotherapy: Costs, Effects, and Public Policy*, Ballinger Publishing Company, Cambridge, Masschusetts.

McLaughlin, C. (1987), "HMO growth and hospital expenses and use: a simultaneous-equations approach," *Health Services Research* 22(2):183–202.

Merrill, J., C. Jackson, and J. Reuter (1985), "Factors that affect the HMO enrollment: A tale of two cities," *Inquiry* 22:388–395.

Newhouse, J. P., and C. E. Phelps (1974), "Price and income elasticities for medical care services," in M. Perlman, ed., *The Economics of Health and Medical Care*, Macmillan, London.

Newhouse, J. P., and C. E. Phelps (1976), "New estimates of price and income elasticities," in R. Rosett, ed., *The Role of Health Insurance in the Health Services Sector*, National Bureau of Economic Research, New York.

Newhouse, J. P., and the Insurance Experiment Group (1993), *Free For All? Lessons from the Health Insurance Experiment*, Harvard University Press, Cambridge.

O'Brien, B. (1989), "The effect of patient charges on the utilization of prescription medicines," *Journal of Health Economics* 8(1):109–132.

Phelps, C. E. (1992), *Health Economics*, HarperCollins, New York.

Phelps, C. E., and J. P. Newhouse (1974), "Coinsurance, the price of time, and the demand for medical care services," *Review of Economics and Statistics* 56:334–342.

Phelps, C. E., S. Hosek, J. Buchanan, et al. (1984), *Health Care in the Military: Feasibility and Desirability of a Closed Enrollment System*, RAND R-3145-HA, Santa Monica, California.

Rice, T., and K. R. Morrison (1994), "Patient cost sharing for medical services: A review of the literature and the implications for health care reform," *Medical Care Review* 51(3):235–287.

Roddy, P. C., J. Wallen, and S. M. Meyers (1986), "Cost sharing and use of health services. The United Mine Workers of America health plan," *Medical Care* 24(9):873–876, September.

Rosett, R. N., and L. F. Huang (1973), "The effect of health insurance on the demand for medical care," *Journal of Political Economy* 81:281–305.

Royalty, A. B., and N. Solomon (1998), "Health plan choice: Price elasticities in a managed competition setting," *Journal of Human Resources* 34(1):1–41.

Scitovsky, A. A., and N. M. McCall (1977), "Coinsurance and the demand for physician services: Four years later," *Social Security Bulletin* 40:19–27.

Scitovsky, A. A., and N. M. Snyder (1972), "Effect of coinsurance on use of physician services," *Social Security Bulletin* 35(6):3–19.

Short, P. F., and A. K. Taylor (1989), "Premiums, benefits, and employee choice of health insurance options," *Journal of Health Economics* 8:293–311.

Simon, G. E., L. Grothaus, M. L. Durham, et al. (1996), "Impact of visit copayments on outpatient mental health utilization by members of a health maintenance organization," *American Journal of Psychiatry* 153(3):331–338.

Simon, G. E., M. VonKorff, and M. L. Durham (1994), "Predictors of outpatient mental health utilization in a health maintenance organization," *American Journal of Psychiatry* 151:908–913.

Smith, Dean (1993), "The effects of copayments and generic substitution on the use and costs of prescription drugs," *Inquiry* 30:189–198.

Taylor, A. K., and G. R. Wilensky (1983), "The effect of tax policies on expenditures for private health insurance," in J. Meyer, ed., *Market Reforms in Health Care*, American Enterprise Institute, Washington, D.C.

Wallen, J., P. Roddy, and S. Meyers (1986), "Male-female differences in mental health visits under cost-sharing," *Health Services Research* 21(2):341–350.

Wedig, G. J. (1988), "Health status and the demand for health," *Journal of Health Economics* 7:151–163.

Weiner, J. (1993), "The demand for physician services in a changing health care system: A synthesis," *Medical Care Review* 50(4):411–449.

Wells, K. B., E. Keeler, and W. G. Manning (1982), "Patterns of outpatient mental health care over time: Some implications for estimates of demand for benefit design," *Health Services Research* 24(6):773–789.

Zweifel, P., and W. G. Manning (2000), "Moral hazard and consumer incentives in health care," in A. J. Culyer and J. P. Newhouse, eds., *Handbook of Health Economics*, Elsevier, New York.